The Appalachian Archive

The Appalachian Archive

───── Robert Morrison Randolph ─────

RESOURCE *Publications* • Eugene, Oregon

THE APPALACHIAN ARCHIVE

Copyright © 2021 Robert Morrison Randolph. All rights reserved. Except for brief quotations in critical publications or reviews, no part of this book may be reproduced in any manner without prior written permission from the publisher. Write: Permissions, Wipf and Stock Publishers, 199 W. 8th Ave., Suite 3, Eugene, OR 97401.

Resource Publications
An Imprint of Wipf and Stock Publishers
199 W. 8th Ave., Suite 3
Eugene, OR 97401

www.wipfandstock.com

PAPERBACK ISBN: 978-1-6667-3387-7
HARDCOVER ISBN: 978-1-6667-2886-6
EBOOK ISBN: 978-1-6667-2887-3

11/05/21

Sections 31–41 of this poem were originally published in *Nimrod International Journal*.

"Let all our employment be to know God: the more one knows Him, the more one desires to know Him."

—*The Practice of the Presence of God*, Brother Lawrence

1

You make of my life
an archive of light and pale-blue pain.

My blood calls Your name out through skin and bone,
like a bird flying out of stone
on translucent wings.

You break my heart with the slightest touch of Your fingertips,
my Lord.

I lie awake in the dark,
almost a stone or star, beyond the flesh of anyone's hands,
traveling thousands of miles an hour inside my body,
trying to comprehend Your love.

Across a huge snowy field,
that black speck entering the trees is my soul
looking for You. And I am nothing, less than old boards
leaning against the barn.

I scream silently;
my mouth hangs open as if anyone could hear into my face,
as if I have opened the last small packet of my breath,

as if trying to name the exact *presence* of You this moment
by using only one vowel.

Your bell tolls behind my ribs, tied to the rope of my blood.

2

The dresser mirror reflects a window
dimly lit with last light and specked with rain. A vase of dark green glass
holds three roses. Shy air blooms around the petals.

There is a voice inside the room's light, a prayer.
A hand mirror lies face up on a handmade doily near a cloisonné
    jewelry box,
casting a small pool of light on the wallpaper,
brightening small gold fleurs-de-lis against the night.

The mirror flows like a river in two worlds as does my heart.
The glass is filled with longing and pain, and knows my name.

The mirror falls into me, as I fall into it,
and I know again my life thus far has been a dream, a residence in
    reflections.
There is softness beyond naming inside the last light of day,
as the room goes dark.

All has been given over;
a silent ordinance prevails beyond the shape of falling rain,
an immense space and pattern in my blood, the best I might ever do
    for a home.

I want to drift into the dark mirror.
Always reflection in glass seems purer to me than its source,
but right now beyond reflection, beyond source, loneliness and distance
seem channels to You, as if I am in love with Your absence, with Nothing.

I want the air I breathe in this night-filled room
to fill my lungs with embodiment from within.

3

I paint the walls white,
because the white resembles absence.
I drive nails into the absence, trying to create a crucified God in my mind.

I think all around the nails, lost.
I stare at my white wall, as if watching a blank movie screen.

I imagine the calmness around the ankles as the body dies.
Moaning from onlookers fills the near air
and the distant air drains through holes in silence.

There is the shape of the cradle his mother's arms make for a baby long gone,
as she watches. Her arms become a dark gate.

I try lifting my hands through his death until my fingers become stars,
but long arcs of pain and golden shadows cast by numbness
pull me back. The dead body is a silent tent, a temple.

We all know he can leave without a trace,
so I imagine myself putting my forehead against his forehead
and closing my eyes.

Even in death, he is a fountain flowing silently.
His voice held an emerald. He spoke best about the air touching his body.
I stop imagining and look at my right hand,
listening to the sad eloquence of my wrist bones, and I ask *who is the one
who never forgets me.*

I confess I do not know.
I reach up and touch the window above my bed.
There, at my fingertips, the glass and I are old friends of my failure,
my reaching.

4

Sometimes memory drifts like mist
between mountain peaks, almost shaping itself into arcs,
the dark world *itself adrift in time.*

Last summer an okra blossom
appeared in my garden, for example; I forget how long it rained,
but I remember going out to see it,
water off my hat brim.

But were You with me that day,
or the next? (I have lived at the foot of Your *silences*
as at the foot of mountains and my longing for You has flown
like a hawk through cloudy and cloudless days
until the hawk dropped from the air.)

I remember the day I thought You sat in Your white dress,
Your white blossoms, as a blooming dogwood
up on the hill. Or, rather, I remember *how I felt* about You,
like somebody rang a temple bell in my blood.

But how small I made You then,
denying the cutting edge of each lovely petal slicing me open
too deeply to feel,

lacerations in my soul I had to reshape myself around,
and, looking back, know there was a giving
beyond what I could carry.

The natural world has painted living landscapes
in my core; drawn for You.

The long reeds by shore lean and whisper,
voiced by eternal wind. Water moves against the stalks.
A net of flotsam rises, falls,
water bending in against the root-ribbed land,
laying a line of leaves and twigs beneath branches of willows,
but it is not You.

The water carries a lineation in its voice,
an edge of desire, as it names itself. It shapes the smallest details
into a fragile story made for its own day, *its own light.*

If I could meet You but briefly,
sitting by a train window,
strangers in a dining car headed south
to the port, and I listening as You speak of love,
lifting a demitasse cup to Your lips
and setting it back on its white saucer
as You lean toward me to whisper,

gold rain streaking the window
and gold strands of water dropping
between the car and distant hills
like a gold net for my heart's core,
as You say one word, just for me,
that breaks my life into two jagged pieces
that I hold wherever I go.

5

The dark day, Jesus dying, his wrists nailed to wood,
his loneliness beyond drawing in ink,
artists across the centuries reaching inside themselves
to find him, across the sky his agony like rain,

agony like a street that leads to the town square
where beggars sit, refugees from the north. I sit with them,
as if in a small room filled with rivers
flowing from the throne of God. The beggars float
in God's waters like unnoticed leaves;

I want to recede into the hollows of my bones
and speak God's name in the marrow,
my voice itself a beggar, nothing more.

I want an ordinary moon in tonight's sky,
lying in a darkness like weeds, a darkness like hair,
to be held by fingertips like a grape;
I want *to know that happened,* without seeing it.

I want the sea to deepen everywhere with a second loneliness,
to lift its marble gloves toward my windows,
to speak its long soliloquy of desire and velvet candle flame,
to make of prayer its fugitive masonry.

6

I wait for You by water, on this park bench by a park pond.
I watch trains come and go.
I watch the dark water in the pines' reflection. I hear mourning doves.

Today white butterflies worked the lavender blossoms,
each flutter of wing a sort of sleep,
almost a season, on the right and on the left, of death,

as though, having given up on any breakthrough,
fragility and need took over, as though beauty instead of sickness
and solitude defined You. The butterflies seemed stones
in perfect hands, ready to be cast against me,
an epiphany, for my sins. It would have been a small, sure death,
death of a hundred pieces, and yet an empty pocket.

7

You are the three channels of Father,
Son and Holy Ghost running in the sea of my heart,
mind, and soul. One sea with three channels--
and my consciousness, like a fish, darts within You, breathing of You.

How can the fish *know* the water; how can I know You?
How can the fish *love* the water; I love You somehow, *because You let me*,
as if the sea permitted its fish to love from the scales,
from the teeth, the element of very existence, the milieu of all being,

but with love so immediate from the body that the mind cannot catch up,
cannot name the presence, and knows the love as loss,
as always grasping, always failing.

I swim in You, breathe You, love You, but cannot know You;
the channels are different and yet one, one sea,
one source and sustenance, one alertness around my body;
I live in Your name, unable to say it,
and not being one with it—in knowing myself first, before knowing You,
in watching myself try.

I want to know You; this life is made of growth around that core failure,
failure to die into You—not to die into death, but die into life.
As if the fish could become the water itself, the water from which it came,
and to move its own body *of* water *through* the water,
as the Father, Son, and Holy Ghost existing through each other.

8

Oh Christ, flesh and bone, and mystery,
union of God and man and wholly each, yet how?
Union with Father and Holy Ghost:
one vine, branch, root, and leaf. A weeping willow
outside my window drapes its slender leaves
like a shroud, a winding cloth around nothing, which is sacred space,
a place of waiting, a presence chamber.

Holy Christ, You are a presence chamber for Yourself,
yet how? Is that the lesson?
Must I be a presence chamber for myself?
Waiting is distance and pain, separation from You.
The pain You must have felt to be named Christ,
and, therefore, axiomatically, distant from Yourself.
The pain of the plant if it could name its parts from within,
when the space under the leaves becomes sacred.

O Lord, surrender is all, giving up language, drifting away
from nouns and verbs, inhabiting relationship only
until both poles fold together, any distinctiveness or special roles
pool, or *the three* become one.

9

This morning my roses flame with secrecy
behind the beauty I can see, as if last night's sunset
fell down through each bloom,

down through the stalk and into the roots,
where a secret sorrow remains as shards of last light,

something to hold deeply
and send back to morning's petals. I too remember what I never knew,
unfolding of dim sorrow every day
behind everyday chores, as if I once knew You well in every heartbeat,

or as if You started my heart beating,
and I forgot You when the movement of blood through my veins
took the place of Your face.
Behind my blood I still feel Your gaze.

10

Fog all night, angelically patient, edgeless,
no Pharos. This morning I watch bare branches dip, wind composing
its perpetual *billet-doux*.

The teakettle spouts a thin, soft cry,
set away from the flame. In the teapot, a jade halo
encircles the silver infuser.

The winter branches mime a phrasing
I long to say, as I add honey and lemon to the poured green tea,
the porcelain cup translucent, a bit blue.

I want to say the Word beyond portrayal and argument,
reason and presentation, beyond time,
the word always "I am," Your name, and in saying to die into being.

You say me into life second by second;
I want to say You, and be who You say I am, to awake
into consciousness of breathing Your breath,
consciousness of the utterance of Being.

11

An edge of rain crosses the river,
a dark drift of gray, like a curtain approaching
the willows. I do not close the window,
but listen to the raspy sound of downpour,
like a hawser being dragged across tin.

Half an hour later I hear the rain fold and unfold,
like someone turning huge pages
of parchment, as the storm drifts away in twilight.
Then stillness remains as if, looking at each other,
we raise loving cups of darkness to our lips.

12

From my house the low hills extend
in all directions, like a field of thought,
an abiding idea aware of itself.

I long to be the knowing and
the known, the verbal heart beating
inside the noun. The fire Moses saw,
destroying systematic theology.

I remember sitting in seminary
twenty two years ago listening to logical
arguments proving Your existence,

and as I listened I looked out the window
at the clouds moving behind bare winter branches,
and I knew the window was also You,
the voice of the teacher, the clouds, the glass
in the window, my mind, all was You,
all Your love, exactly as thick as the fabric of life itself,
and my knowing it was also You.

Now I look at the hills outside my window, foothills actually,
and inexpressible actually,
as all is everywhere inexpressible, at once, and all is You
saying Your name to Moses, who is also You,
or saying Your name to me.

These hills, rich with deer trails
and hawk nests, at sundown fall into themselves,
creating a huge dark silence, like a dark room
that holds all things, even angels, and the absence of angels.

I lie in bed, looking out my window
feeling the pain of night. The stars seem victims of my love for You.
I make them distant fires saying what I want your name to be.

The weight of the stars *pouring* into my eyes,
claims all authority for a moment, as though I have been *asked for*
from the night sky.

13

I am in Greece in 1994, on Lesbos,
watching the sea open and close its hands.

Uphill behind me a white horse grazes.
Octopus fishermen work the shallow rocks just offshore.

One calls out to me, asking what time it is. I tell him,
and wonder why it matters.
The small waves break against the rock I sit on,
which is white.

I close my eyes and feel the sun on my body
and I feel the whiteness enter me
from the rocks. It is as if I have spread out, opened up,
received meaning beyond naming,
joined a whiteness wider than perspective. My heart and blood
turn white, and I sit still

feeling solitary, yet gathered in. I slow my thoughts,
trying to give myself only to the moment,
hoping it is You, but it is not. It is only the white of everything
wanting to claim me just then, and it lets me go again
as I open my eyes.

Unlike Paul, I heard no voice,
only the quiet lapping of the water and the easy breeze,
and I thought I had made all the meanings myself,
but I know finally I cannot make anything, and all belongs
to You. So thank You for letting the white
out of itself and letting it hold me.

14

At times the world seems made of outlines,
a truer reality flowing through everything, like wind
through a net. Those two wood ducks flying across the gray sky

seem inked onto rice paper, their flight marking
an edge of something, and my eyes watching them marking
another edge. Between us blows a hunger to know You,

and come into new being made of that knowing.
Sometimes the mountains themselves seem marks on paper
left by an unseen artist's hand;

this world, these rivers and rocks, are shaped from hunger and fear,
and Your love lives inside it all,
without distance, like the taste of ripe fruit.

15

The hawk flies along the shoreline, rebuilding any loss
of hawk within any rock, or so it seems.

I feel such rapport between the wings, the proud head carried
into the wind, and the water softly lapping the shore
that they seem one brush stroke,
or one bow moved across tuned strings.

The rocks seem to wait for the hawk,
and the heavy heart of the flying bird to fall through them, to weight them
truly and appropriately,
to give them their essential place.
The heart of the hawk falls
through everything as it flies overhead.

You are here, building this moment whose width knows no boundary,
what I see but part of all enacted right now,
everywhere in all universes. All of You falling through all of You,
and all consciousnesses and hungers and knowings
falling through all: Being brought to Being, by the movement of Being,
the Word as gesture.

It seems an identity rests on the water of the lake, about an inch or two high,
all the way across to the far shore, a width of intimation.
I imagine Grace like that, a thin loving response afloat on all the waters
    of the world,
drawn up by love into a secret rain that enters our hearts.

16

I stop for the night, on the way to a conference.
In my motel room,
olive wallpaper covered with golden roses
makes green the evening light, suggesting
patina on the wood desk top,

like the patina on the saddle my father left
in the tack room. Too old and worn to sell, the saddle rested
balanced atop a stall wall
catching some sunlight, gathering dust.

The old barn leaned too far past plumb
one day, and fell. The roof, devoted to one
purpose, kept the ground it covered
dry. I threw the saddle away

when we sold the weathered wood and cleared
the space. But in this rented bed between Blacksburg
and Bluefield, I remember
that saddle under my fingertips,

dust motes falling in the empty stalls,
as I tried to find myself in that space where horses
waited for my father. I stood by myself
by his saddle, and felt shaped by his loss,
resembling all life reaching for You.

17

I make tea.
Wind plays the trellis like a harp,
and acorns hit the cabin's tin roof. I count spaces
as night falls.

Around midnight, rain hits the windows.
And there is a third thing between the glass and the water:
it is Jesus walking on the sea.

18

Just after dawn I canoe
on Ironwood Lake. Dogwoods bloom in the hills,
among pines and hickories.

The light seems to build itself
out from my body, like a paragraph
whispered by my skin. Inside me, a holy
silence presses against my heart.

My father, also, loved to canoe.
I have seen the day extend from his fingers
closed on the neck of a paddle, the light of his body
reaching houses built on the sides of the hills
around the lake, softening barns.
Even now there remains for me a lingering light he left behind.

We all carry light
given by You, a glow from the created blood
that began in Adam, a river
still flowing from that spring. My father who moved his consciousness
into his blood, trying to know You,
lived softly. He liked to watch a lake surface dimple
with feeding trout, like gentle whisperings
from another world.

19

This world consists of desire.
Fog comes in, to me a sacrament, a love.

The cover that conceals the shoreline pines
wants to be human, to bring its gray
grace to our consciousness. The fog is not numbness,
nor is it a mirror, it lives its own vital life.
Let me reach into the fog to touch Your body.

20

I walk in the park
under bare sugar maples that have entered
their devoted winter silence.
It is November.

I can feel an unsayable darkness
next to the bark. I bow my head and pray,
touching the one limb
I can reach.

I close my eyes. The dark
behind my eyelids is this life
of separation from You,
unlike the tree's unbrokenness.

21

I do not long for permanence,
only clarity—nearness to Your creativity—
immersion in Process without guideline or outline
meaningful to me.

Sorrow grows inside each stone, like an idea
the stone has come to believe, like a pale blue flame or autumn sky
in the stone's core. One can feel the distance within stones
walking among them by the sea.

Hunger is all, desire,
broken into the things of this world. A clear flame burns
everywhere, the flame of distance from You.

Sometimes all I know and all I feel
comes to a sharp edge, a sense of selfhood so strong
I want to turn my back to the world, and I want to cut with all I am
through to You, to slip, then, away,
sharper, sharper, *sharp beyond all edges*, then to nothing,
to width and fading, to *perhaps a pale blue flame*,
a clarity—to some primordial motion
behind the formation of a verb not yet spoken.

And yet, You reach toward Yourself in me.
You are *here*, reaching,
being me—being this world,
being all I know
and think.

Knowing that—and yet not knowing You inside You,
I write this archive of sorrow,
the voice of a mirror.

22

I sit on a balcony reading,
watching the Aegean. One bird
heads out over the water, a soliloquy.

A priest walks past, dark robe,
snow white beard, wild hair.
He walks with a staff.

In his thick hand, the thin wood
seems to have just arrived
in this world. He passes

behind a flowering almond,
thickly black behind the sheer white.
He seems to use just part of the alphabet,

maybe the slopes of a few letters.
Even so, I feel the shape of his passing,
which seems a profound tenderness,

a gesture beyond duplication.
But he seems to have forgotten
to pay attention to the sea he carries in his blood,

the sea I also carry,
as if he does not feel the waves stirred by Your hand
unfold on the shoreline of every breath.

23

O God, can You be broken, hurt,
in Your love for me? It is not the true answer I want,
but the one I long for, as a lover. John says,
"Jesus wept." How often have You wept for me?

We reach toward each other,
except that You also reach with my heart toward Yourself,
as I grasp only the images I make of You.

If I could enter the current of Your love,
know Your tenderness and pain,
I believe I would surely die by knowing your kiss,

and then by breaking up into a thousand children
whose bodies fade into flames of joy
then fade away.

At times my consciousness seems like a tree bark
aware only of itself,
protecting something indispensably serious just past knowing,
out of reach inside me, a deep love and sorrow
whose existence is also my limitation,
my bounded, finite work of enclosure.

24

As I kneel at my parents' headstone,
a blue jay carves its cry
into the smoothed and polished granite
so shallowly and temporarily it can be felt as a breeze,
but not seen.

My soul knows birdsong carved in stone,
Your language enacted in,
and enacting,
this world. My soul wants to know
all that can be said,
the whole meaning of the primordial Word;

my soul rises and falls like the sun,
like a wave coming from afar, breaking apart
against the edge of its native country.

I think of my parents in a small boat
sailing under my knees, under the ground, on vacation, my father at the tiller,
my mother reclining on deck, happy in their deaths.
I call them into that image, I wish them it,
and thank You for letting me build that image
alongside my grief.

Such is Your love,
the hope that arose in the separation of water from water,
the hope that arose in the space made for human life,
in human consciousness

which is inextricable from separation and duality,
and therefore imbued
with loneliness. Hope inhabits my longing,

a longing for reconnection with You
I feel bone deep when I watch rain fall on the sea.

25

Is there a nuclear thread of knowing
woven into the fabric of being, a *Way* in Being
that is You, as the bible says?

And are there other ways in Being?
Is all the rest of the fabric sentient, lost, and lonely—
all Being making one cloth of varying dimensions of lesser
 consciousness,
all lonely around the core thread of meaning,
which is You?

When the cloth folds, do You fold too?
Do You share the horrors of terrorism, the effects of war on children,
of epidemics, disasters, because You are in the fabric?
Is the fabric woven at all only because You are of it,
weaving it?

Today I imagine myself a thread in a fabric
in which the weaver has entered the cloth in fact, as another thread,
one made of light, perhaps,
or of a feeling—love—
a thread made of love, nonetheless a thread,

and I long to be that deepest dimension of the cloth of which I am a part,
the part that, weaving itself,
weaves everything else as well.

At best, there is a glow of awareness
I feel from sensing my immersion in the wholeness of the weaving,
and there are pockets of light created by nature,

and there is art, the candle-like flame burning itself out throughout
    the tapestry,
splendid, and true in its self-reference—if the fabric
could exist without You, the art-fire of human self-consciousness
    would be all
that were possible.

But, finally, above all, inside the darkness
there is the thread of eternal light that cannot be made, but is.

This thread can have no weight,
creating a cloth into which *a way of light* is woven,
and in which the light does the weaving,
a cloth making itself,

and today I imagine myself a thread in *that fabric*.
Something seemingly absent
holds everything together around me.

26

My sense of awe about being woven into a tapestry beyond comprehension
seems to call forth an alertness and love
from the unimaginable entirety of the fabric,
a response from the spirit of the whole cloth, a holy spirit.

Sometimes this sense of being *noticed*,
loved by all that is,
carries a paradoxical sense of transparency,
as if I am called to diminishment of self,
to some drastic measure of sacrifice.

I am driving the old pickup along the river.
My wife and I talk about the hawks and dogwoods.

She opens the thermos and pours a cup of tea.
There seems to be a consciousness, like an animal made of air,
in the air around her face, looking at me as she looks down at her tea.

The animal of air loves her.
The life of the moment,
like a deep dream, always offers the heart's understanding,
and in this moment I see I am only the dreamer, although wide awake.

The air by her skin is sincere, as if reciting a holy text
which is her body. What is it that lives by us our whole lives,
    if not the Holy Spirit?

27

There is steadiness in reciting the same prayer,
lonely and glasslike, like a vase. It is like keeping a jar full of rain
in order to feel calm. My infant daughter sleeps in her crib
in a dark room, except for slatted light on the wall
from a Venetian blind. I stroke her hair.
We are both made of slowed down light, as is everything.
In truth, all things are relationships.

In the country of my heart, I travel by hot air balloon
because of her. At the speed of light, the cage becomes the bird.
Any prayer I can say could only be a container.

28

To the north, across the valley, the lights of town
seem false, and to the west, in the meadow, the oaks and hickories
seem dark and thoughtful.

Everything around me seems developed from the past,
as if I am in a dark photograph.

A warm wind blows in
from the edge of something enormous, an air mass over Ohio,
and something small, the speed limit sign on Rolling Meadows Road.
Everything You make is necessary,
everything folds into itself while reaching outward.

Life is a strange jar,
made of mortality but filled with forever.
Sometimes it seems You come toward me, then flow around me like a stream
around a rock. I want there to be, instead,
one flame with you.

29

I'm sitting in a small church
on the banks of the Monongahela River.
In the last flood year, water reached the steps
before turning back.

When You entered Yourself as Christ Jesus,
did you fold further into Yourself, away from me?

The bible says You were well pleased with Jesus,
your son; and Jesus says You sent him;
but he felt forsaken at death, *forsaken*, as though distance existed
within You, as though the sea forsook the shoreline.

On the cross Jesus looked into himself
as though holding a mirror up to his face, and saw only his skin,
the loneliness in human being.

Can that be felt without desire? At that moment did duality become real
inside You, causing rejection of us in self defense,
causing the thread of light to encyst itself inside the fabric of being,
or did Jesus, the Word, rebuild it all at that moment of love
    and despair on the cross,
in effect take dominion of all heaven and earth?

Was human being rebuilt from inside itself,
that is to say, did You focus *Yourself* around our cry for your presence?
Was hunger for you built into every flowing stream,
every bird's flight? And is there counterbalancing joy embedded deep
    in the cry,
softening it, as though Jesus himself remains with us?

I watch the two candles burn on the altar of this small church,
one set on either side of the offering table. Duality circumscribes
    human consciousness,
even if there is one fire. As if each candle
can only see the flame in the other.

30

I watch ducks fly across a gray sky
on a cold day, and the whole world seems made
for a brooding, private, reason

like a house full of clear mirrors.
I feel the weight of Your love in my heart,
and for that instant it feels like hope,

as though You hope for something from me!
And *your hope* carries something like trust or faith in me,
    which floods my heart
with mystery, loneliness, and abiding joy.

31

    A heron stands in the shallow pool,
  alone,
past the solitude of the white rose in its vase,
past the stillness of the split-rail fence darkened by morning dew,
    past the wood
  now smooth with light, past the fragile shadows where chair legs
touch the back porch.

The river looks away,
    like snow that stops falling,
and the bird lifts into the clear sky, down the valley, *a leaf*
    floating in a bowl.

I sit in a Shaker chair,
bare feet on a hardwood floor, drinking tea by a window.

Sometimes my heart
is a black coffer, gathering beauty, hoarding structure, in search of
  transcendence.
Forgive me my idolatry.

32

This morning
    I waited out the rain under a pine,
then set out. I felt hard to find, walking the wet path home, small,
        only moving, not being.

    The creek ran like fire at my side,
and praised itself deeply,
    full of feeding trout.
        Blessed One, keep my body open. May I carry circles of air
    in my cupped hands,
and this body seal itself inside Your light.

    The floating absence pervading the visible,
an absence heavy as rain,
        may it anchor my bones in Your deep,
    sweet fire.

33

    The end of April,
dogwoods bloom
and poise to fade. The creek below my cabin,
filled with thaw and moonlight,
riffles *sotto voce*.

The granite bluff seems sad, silent, disguised,
    made of longing

        turned to stone. May it be broken down
again, and released into birds, to its inner life.

34

    I found a rusted penknife in a long rain,
        blade open,
near Swanson's Eddy—maybe lost by
            a fisherman.

        It seemed a prayer, a hard life, saying itself.
Everything reaches for You.

    I laid the knife on a shelf in my shed,
near a window.

The corroded blade
        and pane of glass form a correspondence,
    an abiding trust.

Perhaps all things
are flowing rivers, made of honesty, flowing home. The rusted steel,
window glass,
      and April rain
          may be the black water of Your blood, setting things just ajar,
enough to unlock this one door—

Forgive me, I wait for deliverance.

35

A finch
flits from twig to twig,
    almost invisible in the sassafras tree,
driven by arrivals
in denial of destination. So it goes,
I go, called to the incidental,
    until nightfall

    when Pennsylvania
        rolls into the earth's shade
and the creek seems to weigh more, cut deeper, to remember.

36

Every day I drink from the spring just downhill, to correct my body's distance
                          from the past,
                from my father
    who showed me that cold water,
        who hung a tin cup on a branch for anyone thirsty on the
        creek path,

and I am sometimes called home in dreams,
    feeling the presence of both my parents, long gone; all seems real,
honest,
distant from You.

37

I have a black and white photograph of my parents on their wedding day,
    from 1939.
They stand, looking serious,
        facing the lens, the next branch.

        I hung the photograph near the kitchen window,
so I can look at them
    and down at the water in the creek,
the flowing testimony of the hills.

    The distances between the photograph
and my skin, and my skin
and the creek,
    are equal lengths of my desire for You,
the shape
of Your absence between arrivals.

38

    I am coming into the distances between us:
the deer seem always
        to ring interior temple bells as they run;
a white oak flies across a gray sky;
the river flows with its birds; *gone*
    say the pines. A gibbous moon rides
        the river's current.

39

Leaves made of farewell drop
into the poor
    water, knowing how it feels.
The moon looks into a silver-framed mirror.

    The river falls between the mountain peaks
        through blossoming dogwoods. In the rain
the white sail of Your absence,
    cold as the whisper of stars.

40

      I sweep the floor again,
looking for the borderline
of my breath. I watch my shirts blow on the clothesline:

    Now all I want
is a clean heart with one river
      running through it, but will I see You?

        Clouds come down into the tall grass
          and no one understands. The lace curtains hold a stranger.
We drink together

    to the moon, that sad jar of light,
and to the river,
        gone still as glass.

41

    Blessed One,
broken and beautiful,
flowers hold
      Your name in their slender throats.

      Your silhouette arises in falling rain,
lit from behind this world,
    Your shadow casts a veil, and then Your eyes
appear here in the same plane with me,
and I feel Your gaze
in the rain.

Thank You for Your love, always unfolding
    itself and unfolding me.

        The stars lift their white hands to You,
the stones lift their small cups. An owl
    calls from far away, a round yellow sound,
            as if its bones were made of amber.

www.ingramcontent.com/pod-product-compliance
Lightning Source LLC
Chambersburg PA
CBHW061302040426
42444CB00010B/2473